Gospel Light's

AGES

BIG BOOK OF PRESCHOOL PUZZLES #2

156 Fun-to-Do Bible Puzzles

- Helps teach Bible stories and Bible verses
- Includes Challenge Puzzles for kindergartners
- Mazes, matching, codes and more

Gospel Light

Reproducible!

CD-ROM INCLUDED

Guidelines for Photocopying Reproducible Pages

Gospel Light's

BIG BOOK OF PRESCHOOL PUZZLES #2

Editorial Staff

Senior Managing Editor, Sheryl Haystead • **Senior Editor,** Deborah Barber • **Writer,** Carol Eide
Editorial Team, Mary Davis, Janis Halverson, Lisa Key • **Contributing Editor,** Sarah Richter
Designer, Annette Chavez

Founder, Dr. Henrietta Mears • **Publisher,** William T. Greig • **Senior Consulting Publisher,**
Dr. Elmer L. Towns • **Senior Editor, Biblical and Theological Content,** Dr. Gary S. Greig

Contents

The Big Book of Preschool Puzzles #2 CD-ROM

On the CD-ROM you will find all the puzzles in the *Big Book of Preschool Puzzles #2*. There are also 52 Bonus Bible Verse Puzzles and a Sentence Strip Page.

Bonus Bible Verse Puzzles

Bible Verse Puzzle 1 (Acts 17:24)

Bible Verse Puzzle 2 (Genesis 1:31)

Bible Verse Puzzle 3 (Colossians 4:2)

Bible Verse Puzzle 4 (1 John 4:14)

Bible Verse Puzzle 5 (Ephesians 2:10)

Bible Verse Puzzle 6 (Deuteronomy 6:18)

Bible Verse Puzzle 7 (Colossians 3:23)

Bible Verse Puzzle 8 (1 Chronicles 29:13)

Bible Verse Puzzle 9 (Deuteronomy 27:10)

Bible Verse Puzzle 10 (Luke 6:31)

Bible Verse Puzzle 11 (Psalm 119:42)

Bible Verse Puzzle 12 (Psalm 4:3)

Bible Verse Puzzle 13 (Matthew 22:39)

Bible Verse Puzzle 14 (John 3:16)

Bible Verse Puzzle 15 (Isaiah 9:6)

Bible Verse Puzzle 16 (Luke 2:10-11)

Bible Verse Puzzle 17 (Zephaniah 3:17)

Bible Verse Puzzle 18 (Psalm 86:11)

Bible Verse Puzzle 19 (Psalm 34:14)

Bible Verse Puzzle 20 (John 1:34)

Bible Verse Puzzle 21 (Matthew 4:19)

Bible Verse Puzzle 22 (Psalm 31:7)

Bible Verse Puzzle 23 (Job 22:27)

Bible Verse Puzzle 24 (Matthew 19:14)

Bible Verse Puzzle 25 (Psalm 86:5)

Bible Verse Puzzle 26 (Psalm 18:1)

Bible Verse Puzzle 27 (1 Chronicles 16:34)

Bible Verse Puzzle 28 (1 Thessalonians 5:15)

Bible Verse Puzzle 29 (Psalm 7:17)

Bible Verse Puzzle 30 (1 Timothy 6:18)

Bible Verse Puzzle 31 (Psalm 147:1)

Bible Verse Puzzle 32 (Matthew 28:7)

Bible Verse Puzzle 33 (2 Corinthians 9:15)

Bible Verse Puzzle 34 (Revelation 1:18)

Bible Verse Puzzle 35 (Mark 16:15)

Bible Verse Puzzle 36 (Psalm 105:2)

Bible Verse Puzzle 37 (Psalm 119:17)

Bible Verse Puzzle 38 (Galatians 6:10)

Bible Verse Puzzle 39 (Proverbs 17:17)

Bible Verse Puzzle 40 (Joshua 1:9)

Bible Verse Puzzle 41 (2 Thessalonians 3:13)

Bible Verse Puzzle 42 (Romans 12:13)

Bible Verse Puzzle 43 (John 13:34)

Bible Verse Puzzle 44 (Genesis 33:11)

Bible Verse Puzzle 45 (Genesis 26:24)

Bible Verse Puzzle 46 (Philippians 4:19)

Bible Verse Puzzle 47 (Jeremiah 10:6)

Bible Verse Puzzle 48 (Hebrews 13:6)

Bible Verse Puzzle 49 (Psalm 31:6)

Bible Verse Puzzle 50 (Luke 11:28)

Bible Verse Puzzle 51 (Psalm 27:11)

Bible Verse Puzzle 52 (Titus 3:1)

How to Use the *Big Book of Preschool Puzzles #2*

Welcome to the *Big Book of Preschool Puzzles #2*, a learning adventure for the preschoolers in your home or classroom. Your preschooler will be excited to review Bible stories and verses through completing mazes, dot-to-dots, What's Different? picture puzzles, matching and counting activities, hidden pictures and a variety of other enticing puzzles.

The Bible puzzles contained in this book teach Bible stories and verses in an age-appropriate way for preschoolers. The puzzles highlight 52 Bible stories and verses, with three puzzles for each Bible story and/or verse. One of the puzzles adds a challenge that is appropriate to challenge kindergarten learners. All of the puzzles will engage your older preschooler and provide a springboard for Bible learning.

How to Use This Book in Your Classroom

Use this book as a fun way to review Bible stories and verses and to practice emerging academic skills. These puzzles can also provide "something more" for older children in your preschool or kindergarten group.

Follow these easy steps for successful use of the puzzles.

1. Before class:

- Find the puzzle(s) that matches your lesson's Bible story or verse: use the contents or one of the indexes.

- Select one or more puzzles to use.

- Photocopy the puzzle(s) you have selected. Make one copy of the selected puzzles for each child, plus a few extras for visitors or for children who want to start over.

- Check the puzzle's directions and Bonus Idea for any extra materials you will need. In addition to pencils, some puzzles may require crayons, scissors and/or glue sticks.

> **Note:**
> If you are using this book along with Gospel Light's *Little KidsTime Growing with God* course, the appropriate puzzles (three per lesson) are designated on the last page of each lesson in the leader's guide.

2. In class:

- Give a pencil and puzzle to each child. Read the puzzle directions aloud.

- Assist children as needed to complete the puzzle. Be ready to explain the Bonus Idea to children as they finish the main puzzle activity.

> For Bonus Ideas that involve writing, print out and photocopy the Sentence Strip Page available on the CD-ROM.

- Talk with children during and after their puzzle work. Your conversation can tie the children's work to the Bible story and verse presented in each puzzle. The printed copy on each puzzle will help you communicate the important link between a Bible story and verse and the everyday lives of your children.

How to Use This Book in Your Home

This book gives you a wonderful opportunity to help your child learn what the Bible says about loving God and following Him every day. You can use the puzzles in this book to talk about Bible stories and verse, and to reinforce emerging academic skills.

Follow these steps for a fun and valuable time of learning and togetherness.

1. Gather the materials needed for the puzzles.

- For most puzzles, nothing more than a pencil is necessary. Crayons, scissors and/or a glue stick are needed for a few puzzles.

- You may want to buy your child a set of colored pencils to use in completing and coloring each puzzle.

The Bonus Idea at the bottom of each puzzle often involves a drawing activity. Suggest your child complete Bonus Idea activities on the back of each puzzle, or provide extra paper for this.

> For Bonus Ideas that involve writing, print out and photocopy the Sentence Strip Page available on the CD-ROM.

2. Keep the *Big Book of Preschool Puzzles #2* in a special place.

- Get out the book and invite your child to work on several puzzles a week.

- Even if your child wants to hurry through the book, encourage him or her to complete only one or two pages at a time, so you can take time to review the Bible verse and Bible story presented in the puzzles.

3. Review the puzzles together to increase understanding.

- Sit with your child to find and read the puzzle's Bible verse in the Bible. Allow your child to highlight the verse in the Bible.

- Read the verse again at bedtime as reinforcement.

- Briefly talk with your child about the life-application ideas presented in the puzzles and about the responses appropriate to your child's own life. Tell how you obey the verse, too.

- As your child completes the puzzles, look back together at the puzzles he or she has finished. Review the Bible stories and verses.

This Bible learning time at home will create a solid foundation for your child as he or she begins to read the Bible for him- or herself. The hours spent on the puzzles and Bible learning will help you and your child build a relationship that will be remembered long after the puzzles are all completed.

Academic Skills and the *Big Book of Preschool Puzzles #2*

Because the *Big Book of Preschool Puzzles #2* is primarily for older preschoolers, these puzzles were created to challenge and aid pre-kindergartners and kindergartners in the acquisition of the same academic skills they are learning. The puzzles in the *Big Book of Preschool Puzzles #2* use the same number, alphabet, logic, spatial and visual identification skills children are being taught in their pre-kindergarten and kindergarten classrooms. And all this is occurring while the puzzles reinforce biblical values and review important Bible stories and verses.

On page 221 of this book, you will find an index that categorizes puzzles according to academic skills. Because of the wide variance in the skill level of all preschoolers (depending on location, preschool attendance and knowledge of English as a first language), the Bible Story and Bible Verse puzzles attempt to hit the median range. The Challenge puzzles are designed for children with more advanced skills.

Your guidance will be an important part of helping your child succeed at the puzzles. Use the tips and hints below.

If the puzzles seem too difficult for your preschooler:

- Avoid using the Challenge puzzles.

- Go over the directions one-on-one with the child. Have the child complete the first step as you watch and encourage him or her.

- Point out the visual helps included on the page (number lines, alphabet lines or dotted example lines to trace).

- In later puzzles, some of these visual helps no longer appear because the majority of preschoolers have internalized these skills. Write a simple number line or dotted example for a child who is still struggling.

- Leave pressure to perform out of the activity. If a puzzle seems too frustrating, give the child a blank sheet of paper and a hint about something to draw that is related to the Bible story or life-application idea. This will leave the child more eager to attempt a puzzle next time.

If the puzzles seem too easy for your preschooler:

- Use the Challenge puzzles more often than the Bible Story or Bible Verse puzzles.

- Point out and read the Bonus Idea to a child who quickly completes a puzzle. Be available to do this as soon as a child is finished with the main puzzle in order to retain the child's interest.

- To extend the child's involvement, invite a child to tell you about his or her Bonus Idea drawing or puzzle creation.

- For an extra challenge, add your own Bonus Idea for children to complete by incorporating specific skills you know your child is working on.

- Be realistic about the time allotted to these puzzle book activities. Do not expect kindergartners to be engaged in a pencil and paper activity longer than 7 to10 minutes.

The best learning occurs when an attentive adult is available to answer questions, guide conversation and activity, and be a real, live model of the biblical values these puzzles teach.

Tips for Teachers and Parents

1. Create a supply box for children to use with the puzzles. Include the following in the box:

- Pencils and copies of the puzzle(s) you have selected

- Crayons, colored pencils or markers for coloring the puzzles

- Scissors and glue sticks for completion of some puzzles

- Extra sheets of blank paper (or the Sentence Strip Page available on the CD-ROM) for use with Bonus Ideas (if backs of puzzles are not used for this purpose)

2. Be available to participate in the learning process.

- Help children figure out what to do on the puzzle page: read the directions and/or give feedback on their completed work.

- Make sure to read aloud the short sentences that link the puzzle to the Bible story, Bible verse or life-application idea. Help children apply the Bible story or verse to their own lives. For example, children may name specific ways to show God's love by helping friends or family members.

3. Help your children enjoy the puzzles.

- Many preschoolers are naturally drawn to puzzles and mazes. Reinforce this by communicating that completing the puzzles is a fun challenge and is helping them grow into the people God has planned for them to be.

- Use praise and encouragement to motivate a child who is working on a puzzle. For example, "Emily, I see you have circled all the matching objects. Good work!" or "Seth, I can tell you are working hard connecting the numbers on this dot-to-dot!"

- Consider placing a sticker or stamp on each completed puzzle.

- Display completed puzzles on a bulletin board in the classroom or on the refrigerator door at home.

- If a child is not interested in a certain puzzle, tell him or her about the Bonus Idea. If the Bonus Idea fails to interest the child, provide the child with blank paper on which to draw. Challenge the child to draw something about the day's Bible story. For example, for the story of the feeding of the 5,000, challenge a child to draw as many fish as he or she can to cover the page.

- Most children find it easy to occupy themselves by drawing. Even if their artwork does not relate to the Bible story, point out that they are using their God-given gifts of eyes, hands and fingers. Staying positive will help your children to be more willing to try puzzles in the future.

- For Bonus Ideas that suggest writing, expect children to use inventive spelling for most words. Encourage children to express their thoughts without worrying about spelling words correctly.

Count all the different kinds of things God created.
Fill in the chart below.

| 1 | 2 | 3 | 4 | 5 | 6 |

We can thank God for making the sea, the land and the trees. The Bible says, "God made the world and everything in it." (See Acts 17:24.)

BONUS IDEA!   Draw other flowers and stars in the picture.

Draw a line to connect the stars in number order to see what God created first, second, third, fourth and fifth.

God made so many amazing things in our world! The Bible says, "God made the world and everything in it." (See Acts 17:24.)

BONUS IDEA!

Trace the dotted lines to draw a star. Try to draw one of your own.

In each group, draw an ✖ on the one that doesn't belong.

God made all the animals in the world. The Bible says, "God saw all that he had made, and it was very good." Genesis 1:31

BONUS IDEA!

How many fish are there? _____   How many birds are there? _____

Circle the animals that start with a **B**.

What is your favorite animal? The Bible says, "God saw all that he had made, and it was very good." Genesis 1:31

BONUS IDEA! Draw animals God made that start with the same letter your name starts with.

Help Adam find Eve in the garden.

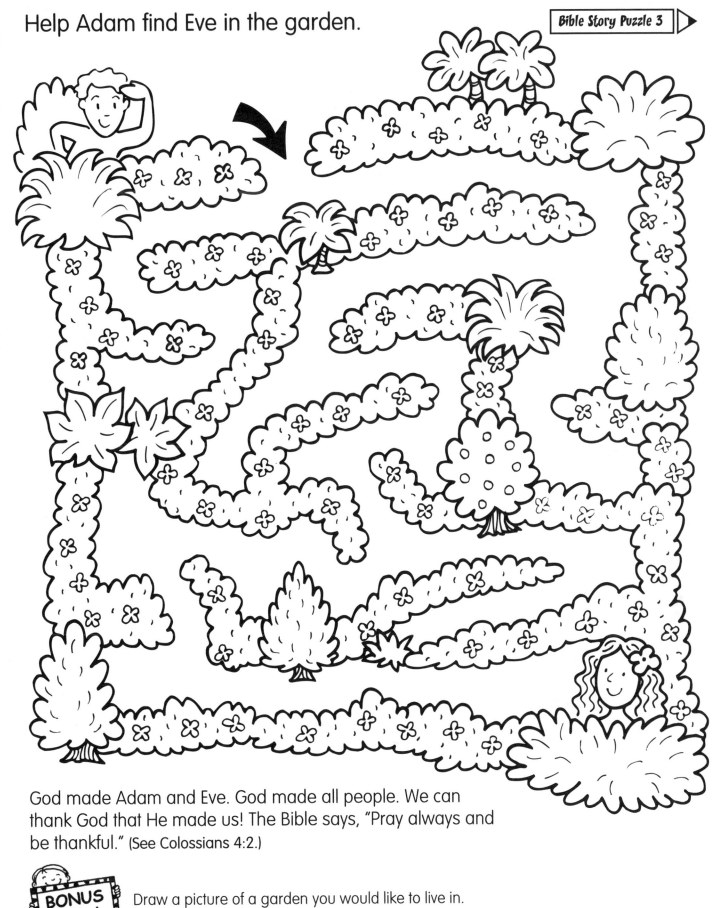

God made Adam and Eve. God made all people. We can thank God that He made us! The Bible says, "Pray always and be thankful." (See Colossians 4:2.)

BONUS IDEA!

Draw a picture of a garden you would like to live in.

Find a hidden letter in each picture. Draw lines to connect each hidden letter with the letter by each child. You will find out who each child is thankful for.

We can thank God for the people who love and care for us. The Bible says, "Pray always and be thankful." (See Colossians 4:2.)

BONUS IDEA!

Think of someone whose name starts with one of these letters: **M**, **B**, **S**. Thank God for that person.

Draw a ◯ around the biggest picture in each row.

God loved Adam and Eve, even when they did wrong. We can thank God for loving us and sending Jesus. The Bible says, "God has sent his Son to be the Savior of the world." (See 1 John 4:14.)

BONUS IDEA!

Make an ✖ on the smallest picture in each row.
Color the middle-sized picture in each row.

Draw a path through the letters to spell "God's Son."

G O E T

Z D V G

H S S O

F K J N

Jesus is God's Son. God showed love for us by sending Jesus. The Bible says, "God has sent his Son to be the Savior of the world." (See 1 John 4:14.)

BONUS IDEA!   Write the name JESUS in the spaces: _____ _____ _____ _____ _____

Connect the dots to see what Noah built.

1 2 3 4 5 6 7 8 9 10 11 12 13 14 15

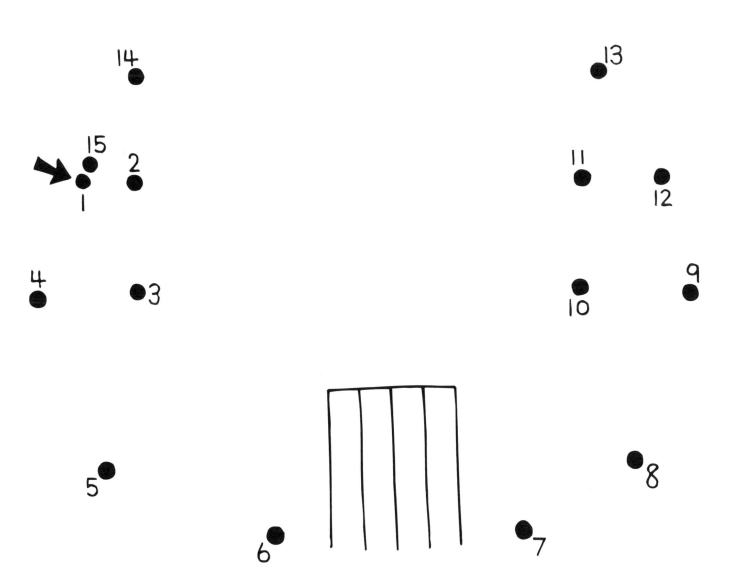

God told Noah to build a boat. Noah obeyed. We can do good and obey God, too. God will help us. The Bible says, "God made us to do good." (See Ephesians 2:10.)

 **BONUS IDEA!** Draw water for the ark to float on. Draw some animals in the ark.

Write the number from the picture in the box that shows a good thing someone can do in each place.

What are the children doing to obey God and do good? The Bible says, "God made us to do good." (See Ephesians 2:10.)

BONUS IDEA!

Cross off all the numbers below to find who helps us do good.

4 2 G 3 o 4 5 d 6 w 7 i 8 9 1 1 5 h e 7 3 1 4 2 p 3 6 u 8 s

In each row, write the missing number on the animal.

1 2 3 4 5 6 7 8 9 10 11 12

God helped Noah get all the animals on the boat. God helps us do good. The Bible says, "Do what is right and good." Deuteronomy 6:18

BONUS IDEA!

Count all the animals on this page. Write that number. _____

Follow the path that shows **R** or **r** to find a child who is doing what is right and good.

God helps us do what is right. The Bible says, "Do what is right and good." Deuteronomy 6:18

Draw a way you can do what is right and good with one of these things.

31

Draw an ✖ on all the silly things in this picture. **Bible Story Puzzle 7** ▷
(There are at least 7.) Draw a ◯ around the people
taking care of the animals.

Noah and his family took care of the animals on the boat. The Bible says, "Whatever you
do, do your work for the Lord." (See Colossians 3:23.)

BONUS IDEA!

How many **pairs** of animals are on the boat?
(A pair is 2 of the same kind.)
Color each **pair** the same color.

These people have jobs that help people.
Go through the maze to match the tools with
the people who use them.

Helping others is a way to show God's love. The Bible says, "Whatever you do, do your
work for the Lord." (See Colossians 3:23.)

BONUS IDEA!

○ the person who wears a ⬚.
□ the person who wears a ⬚.
△ the person you would like to be.

Count the number of objects in each box. Then write the number in the little ☐. Draw a ★ in the box that has **more** than 5 objects. (**More** means a bigger number.)

1 2 3 4 5 6 7 8

God put a rainbow in the sky to remind Noah and his family of God's love and help. They thanked God. We can thank God for helping us, too. The Bible says, "God, we give you thanks." 1 Chronicles 29:13

BONUS IDEA!

Color the rainbows using **more** than 3 colors.
Draw a line between the boxes that have an **equal** number of objects.
(**Equal** means the same.)

Look at the pictures of things we can thank God for.
Draw a ○ around the things that begin with a **B** sound.
Draw a ☐ around the things that begin with a **D** sound.

God helps us and gives us good things. We can thank God for all that He gives us.
The Bible says, "God, we give you thanks." 1 Chronicles 29:13

BONUS IDEA!

Color the **B** pictures BLUE.
Color the **D** pictures RED.
Write the beginning sound next to the leftover pictures.

Help Abraham find his tent.

Abraham obeyed God and went to a new land. We can obey God, too. The Bible says, "Obey the Lord." Deuteronomy 27:10

BONUS IDEA! Color the camel that has black feet.

The children are using these things to obey at the park. Color each one in the picture.

What are the children doing to obey God? We can obey God, too. The Bible says, "Obey the Lord." Deuteronomy 27:10

BONUS IDEA! Count these things in the picture:

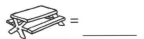 = _____   = _____   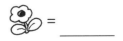 = _____   = _____

Count the animals on each hill.
Then write that number on the shepherd.

1 2 3 4 5 6 7 8 9 10

Abraham and Lot had many animals.
There was not enough food and water for all the animals.
Abraham was kind. He gave Lot first choice of where to live.
We can choose to be kind to others, too. The Bible says, "Do to others as you would have them do to you." Luke 6:31

BONUS IDEA! Find the animal on each hill that is missing a tail. Draw in the tail.

Cut out the pieces. Put the pieces together to show children being kind.

How is someone being kind in the puzzle? Sharing is a way to be kind to others. The Bible says, "Do to others as you would have them do to you." Luke 6:31

BONUS IDEA!

How many of each shape can you find in the picture? Write the numbers on the spaces.

 _____   _____   _____

Draw a line from these objects to where they are in the picture of Abraham and his visitors.

Three visitors said God would give Abraham and Sarah a baby. God kept His promise. We can believe God keeps His promises. The Bible says, "I trust in God's word." (See Psalm 119:42.)

 **BONUS IDEA!** Draw a ◯ around these objects in the picture:

Draw a line through the maze from the ➡ to the ★.

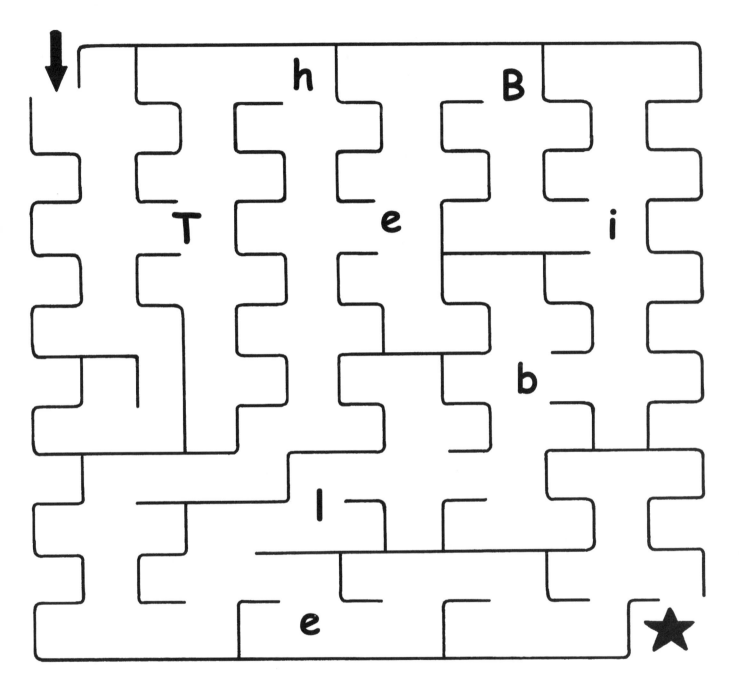

God's promises are written in the Bible. We can believe that God keeps His promises. The Bible says, "I trust in God's word." (See Psalm 119:42.)

Write the letters you passed in the maze on the lines below.

____ ____ ____ ____ ____ ____ ____ ____

51

Color each ◯ you find in this picture of
Eliezer and Rebekah.

How many ◯s are there? _____
Eliezer prayed. God helped Eliezer find Rebekah. We can pray to God, too.
The Bible says, "The Lord hears when I pray to him." (See Psalm 4:3.)

BONUS IDEA!   Draw a ★ by the BIGGEST ◯.

Make a ✔ by the smallest ◯s.

53

Find and circle the letters PRAY in the clock.
We can talk to God by praying any time of the day.

When are some times you might want to pray? We can pray to God anytime. We can thank Him, say we love Him or ask Him for help. The Bible says, "The Lord hears when I pray to him." (See Psalm 4:3.)

BONUS IDEA!

On the blank lines, write the beginning sounds of each picture.
W e   c a n   t a l k   t o   G o d

There are 10 differences between these 2 pictures. How many can you find? Draw an ✖ on a number when you find a difference.

1 2 3 4 5 6 7 8 9 10

Isaac did not argue with the people who wanted his wells. Isaac showed love. We can show love, too. The Bible says, "Love your neighbor." Matthew 22:39

BONUS IDEA!

What do Isaac and his helpers need in order to get water from the well? Draw it in the picture.

Follow the path from the big picture to the little picture that shows a way to show love. What do the letters in the path spell?

_____ _____ _____ _____

We can choose to show God's love. The Bible says, "Love your neighbor." Matthew 22:39

BONUS IDEA!

Write the name of someone you can show love to.

In this picture of the angel talking to Zechariah, how many ◯s can you find? _____

How many □s? _____

How many ▭s? _____

How many △s? _____

The angel told Zechariah he would have a son named John. John would tell the good news that Jesus is God's Son. The Bible says, "God so loved the world." John 3:16

BONUS IDEA!

Write a **c** on each ◯. Write an **s** on each □.

Write an **r** on each ▭. Write a **t** on each △.

These people are all mixed up! Cut the pieces apart and put them in the right places to make three people.

I am glad that God loves everyone! God wants everyone to know about His love. The Bible says, "God so loved the world." John 3:16.

 BONUS IDEA!   Use the pieces to make silly people. How many different silly people can you make?

Find and draw a ⭕ around the numbers 1 to 10 hidden in the picture.

| 1 2 3 4 5 6 7 8 9 10 |

We are glad that Jesus is born! The Bible says, "God's Son is born for us." (See Isaiah 9:6.)

BONUS IDEA!   As you point to each number you found, hold up that number of fingers.

Trace the letters on the cake to find out whose birthday it is.

Jesus is the name of God's Son. Christmas is Jesus' birthday! We are glad Jesus was born. The Bible says, "God's Son is born for us." (See Isaiah 9:6.)

The presents show a pattern. Draw the pattern on these presents.

Complete the dot-to-dots to see who came to visit baby Jesus.

The shepherds told people the good news that Jesus was born. We can tell people the good news, too. The Bible says, "Good news! Today Jesus has been born." (See Luke 2:10-11.)

BONUS IDEA!

Cross off all the numbers below.
Have someone help you read the words that are left. Say the good news together!

| 1 | 2 | J | 3 | e | 4 | 5 | s | u | s | 6 | i | 7 | s | 8 | 9 | b | 5 | o | 2 | 3 | r | n | 4 |

Draw lines between the stars to match each object to a picture of how it can be used to share the good news about Jesus.

The Bible says, "Good news! Today Jesus has been born." (See Luke 2:10-11.)
We can tell this good news to others.

BONUS IDEA!

Count the stars. Write the number. _____
Draw more stars around the pictures.

Trace the path Joseph, Mary and Jesus should take to get to Egypt.

God helped Joseph, Mary and Jesus get to Egypt.
God is always with us and helps us, too. The Bible says,
"The Lord your God is with you." Zephaniah 3:17

BONUS IDEA! Draw a picture of how you would like to travel if you were taking a trip.

○ the object in each row that is the largest.
□ the object in each row that is the smallest.

Where would you find each of these objects? The Bible says, "The Lord your God is with you" Zephaniah 3:17. Which of these places do you like to go? God is with you in that place.

Draw 4 pictures of something at your favorite place (trees, flowers, clouds, etc.). Make each picture bigger than the last one.

What a crowd at the Temple!
Draw a line from Mary and Joseph to Jesus.

Mary and Joseph loved Jesus and helped Him as He grew. God gives people to love and help us grow, too. The Bible says, "Teach me your way, O Lord." (See Psalm 86:11.)

BONUS IDEA!

How many men have striped robes? _____
How many men have something covering their hair? _____

Number the people from the youngest to the oldest.

1 2 3 4 5 6

— — — — — — — — | — — — — — — — — —

God teaches us and cares for us as we grow. The Bible says, "Teach me your way, O Lord." (See Psalm 86:11.) We can thank God for teaching us.

BONUS IDEA! Draw a picture of you as a baby. Then draw what you look like now.

Draw lines to show where these faces are in the picture below.

John told people to do good. Jesus helps us do good. The Bible says, "Stop doing wrong and do good." (See Psalm 34:14.)

BONUS IDEA!

Color a person who looks happy YELLOW.
Color a person who looks angry RED.
Color a person who looks sad BLUE.

Find out what Jesus wants you to do. Color the spaces with ♡s yellow. Color the spaces with ☆s red. Color the spaces with △s blue.

What message did you find? The Bible says, "Stop doing wrong and do good." (See Psalm 34:14.)

BONUS IDEA! What is one good thing you can do to show love for Jesus? Write a sentence about it!

83

In the picture, find and draw a ○ around the letters of Jesus' name.

J E S U S

John baptized Jesus, God's Son. We are glad God sent His Son, Jesus. The Bible says, "Jesus is the Son of God." (See John 1:34.)

 **BONUS IDEA!**

How many letters are in Jesus' name? _____
Draw that number of fish in the river.

Hearing good news makes people feel glad. Look at the set of happy faces in each box. Color the set that has more.

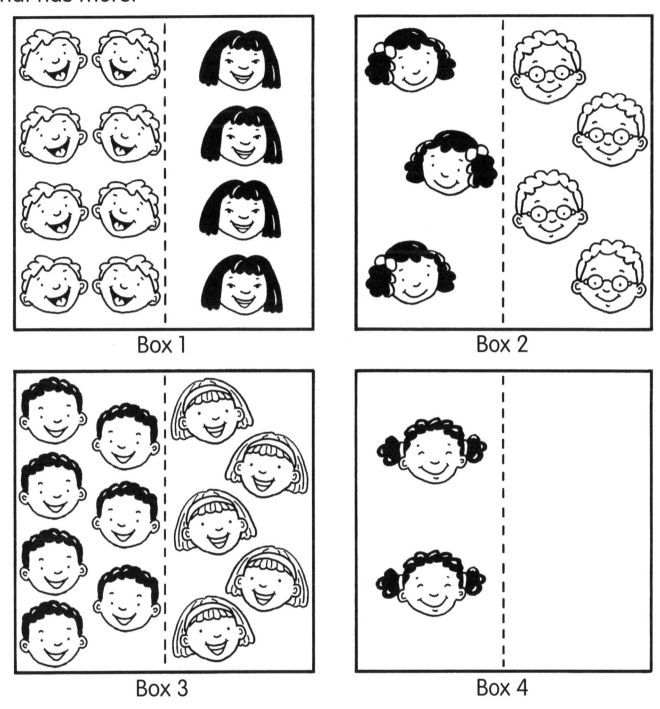

Box 1

Box 2

Box 3

Box 4

The Bible says, "Jesus is the Son of God." (See John 1:34.) This is good news that makes us feel glad.

BONUS IDEA!

Add up the happy faces in each box. Write the numbers below.

Box 1 _____   Box 3 _____

Box 2 _____   Box 4 _____

In each picture, Jesus' helpers are following Him. Are they walking left or right? Draw a ◯ around the correct word under each picture.

← left   right →

left   right

left   right

left   right   left   right   left   right

left   right

left   right

Jesus' helpers followed Him. They learned about Jesus and God's love. We can learn about Jesus and God's love, too. The Bible tells us, "'Come, follow me,' Jesus said."
Matthew 4:19

BONUS IDEA! Draw a picture of yourself following Jesus.
Are you facing left or right? Write **left** or **right** under your picture.

Circle the two footprints in each row that are the same. The matching footprints show ways to learn about Jesus and His love.

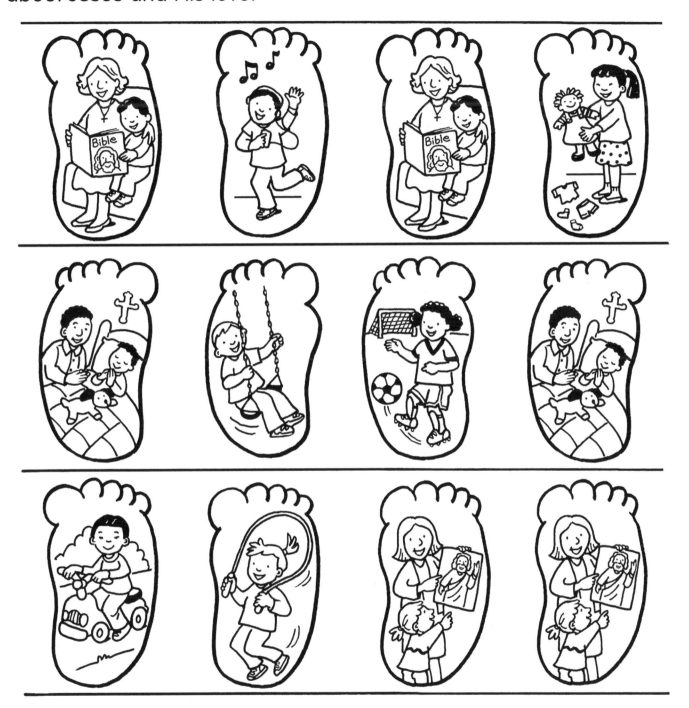

We can learn about Jesus and His love in many ways. When we learn about Jesus we are following Him. The Bible says, "'Come, follow me,' Jesus said." Matthew 4:19

BONUS IDEA! Color the footprints that show ways you like to learn about Jesus.

91

Count each set of objects and write the number.
In each row, draw a ◯ around the set that has
more than the others.

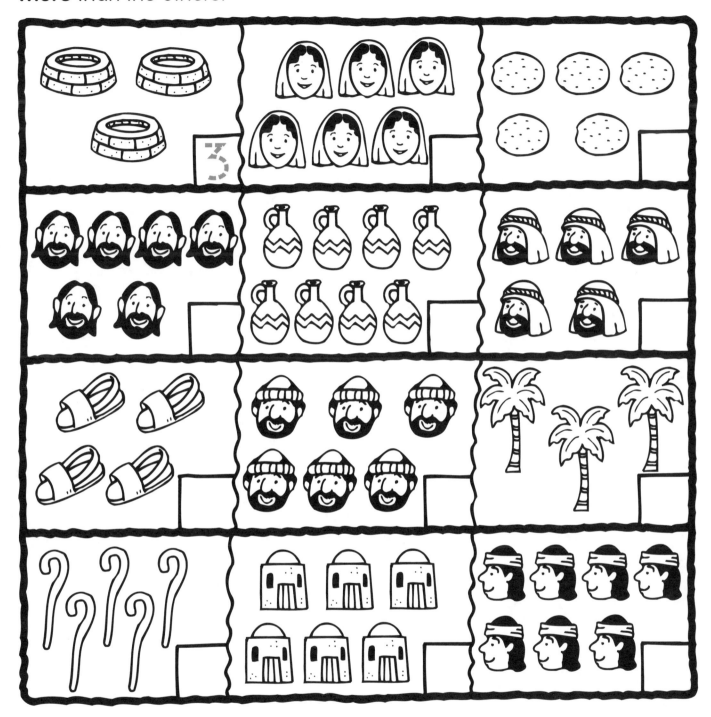

The woman at the well was glad that Jesus loved her. Jesus loves us, too! The Bible says,
"I will be glad and rejoice in your love." Psalm 31:7

BONUS IDEA! In each row, draw an ✖ on some objects so that all sets in that row have the same
number of objects.

Draw an ✖ on every **c**, **e**, **f**, **h** and **k**.

f	k	g	c	c	e	h	k
k	e	h	l	h	f	k	f
e	k	c	e	f	a	f	c
h	f	c	k	c	c	e	d

Write the leftover letters in order on the lines to spell the secret word.

_____   _____   _____   _____

We are glad that Jesus loves us! The Bible says, "I will be glad and rejoice in your love."
Psalm 31:7

BONUS IDEA! Color the children who look like they are glad.

Draw an ✖ on the pictures that are not part of the big picture. Color in the little pictures that are part of the big picture.

Jesus taught His helpers to pray to God. We can pray to God, too. We can tell God we love Him. The Bible says, "Pray to God, and he will hear you." (See Job 22:27.)

BONUS IDEA!

Draw a picture of yourself praying.
Hide the letters **P**, **R**, **A** and **Y** in the picture.
Give your picture to a friend, so your friend can find the hidden letters in it.

○ the word PRAY each time you find it in the word search.

X P R A Y W

W R P R A Y

A A X W P A

R Y P R A Y

When we pray, God listens to us. We can tell God that we love Him. The Bible says, "Pray to God, and he will hear you." (See Job 22:27.)

BONUS IDEA!

What is one thing you can say when you talk to God? We can say thank you to God for everything He has given us. Draw something you are thankful for.

Color in all the spaces with children in them.

What letter did you make? **J** is the first letter in Jesus' name. Jesus loves and cares for you! The Bible tells us, "Jesus said, 'Let the little children come to me.'" Matthew 19:14

BONUS IDEA!

Write your name. Are any letters the same as in Jesus' name?
Practice writing Jesus' name. He loves you!

Follow the footsteps to see who is helping each child. Challenge Puzzle 24 ▷

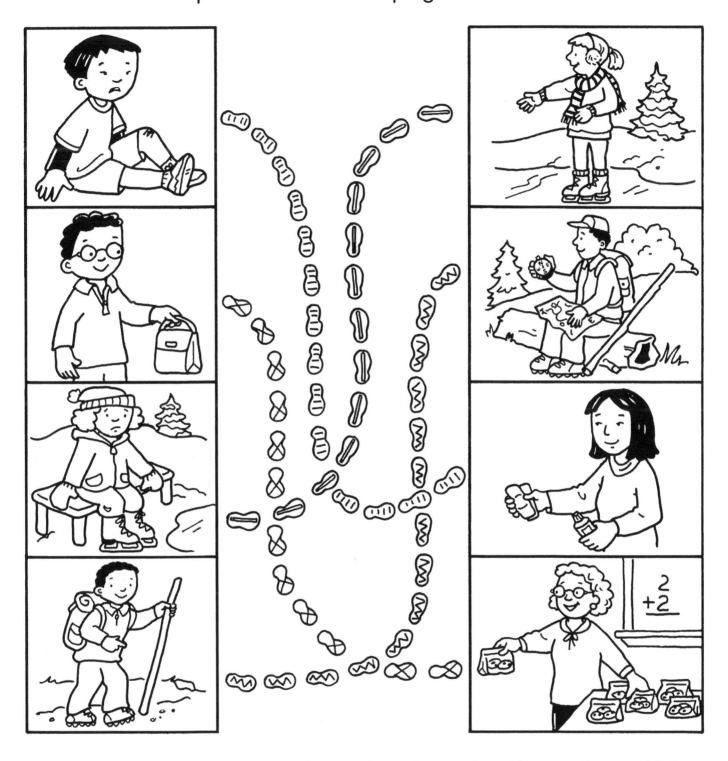

Jesus loves us by giving us people to love and care for us. The Bible says, "Jesus said, 'Let the little children come to me.'" Matthew 19:14

 **BONUS IDEA!**

Color the people with blue.

Color the people with green.

Color the people with  yellow.

Follow the maze through the tree.

Jesus loved Zacchaeus, even though Zacchaeus had done wrong things. Jesus loves us, too, even when we do wrong. The Bible says, "You are kind and forgiving, O Lord." (See Psalm 86:5.)

BONUS IDEA! Look for another way through the tree.

Add numbers to put the pieces in order to make a story about forgiving.

Jesus forgives us when we do wrong. We can love and forgive others. The Bible says, "You are kind and forgiving, O Lord." (See Psalm 86:5.)

BONUS IDEA! Write a sentence that tells about each picture.

In each row, draw the coins that continue the pattern.

    _____ _____

     _____

    _____ _____

 _____ _____

The poor woman gave all the coins she had to show her love to God.
We can show our love to God, too. The Bible says, "I love you, O Lord." Psalm 18:1

BONUS IDEA! Design your own coin.

Cut out the pieces. Put the pieces together to make four pictures that show ways to show love to God.

We can show love to God in many ways. What are the children doing to show they love God? The Bible says, "I love you, O Lord." Psalm 18:1

Draw lines to match the picture to the word that tells about it.

sing

pray

A man asked Jesus to make his son well.
Help the man get back home to see his son.

Jesus loved the man and his son. Jesus loves and teaches us about God's love, too.
The Bible says, "Give thanks to the Lord. His love is forever." (See 1 Chronicles 16:34.)

The Bible says the son got better at the exact time Jesus said he would get better.
What time do these clocks show?

Draw a clock that shows 3:00.

_____   _____   _____

Count the boxes next to each item to see which one is the tallest. Circle the tallest item.

God shows His love by caring for us. What are some things God gives us to show His love? The Bible says, "Give thanks to the Lord. His love is forever." (See 1 Chronicles 16:34.) We can thank God for his love.

BONUS IDEA! Draw pictures that begin with the same sound as each letter in your name. Draw a ★ next to a picture that shows something God gives to show His love.

Draw a ◯ around the picture in each row that has something missing.

Four kind men brought their friend to see Jesus. We can be kind to others, too. The Bible says, "Always try to be kind to each other." 1 Thessalonians 5:15

BONUS IDEA!

Below each letter write the letter that comes after it in the alphabet.

j	h	m	c

You can spell **kind**!
Find and draw a ◯ around that word in the Bible verse.

Draw a line through the maze from START to someone being kind.

Jesus teaches us to be kind to others. The Bible says, "Always try to be kind to each other."
1 Thessalonians 5:15

BONUS IDEA!

◯ pictures in the maze that begin with the letter **T**.

When Jesus made these men well, only one man thanked Him. Draw a ◯ around the man who thanked Jesus:

1. His arms are above his head.
2. He is wearing sandals.
3. He is smiling.

We can thank Jesus, too. The Bible says, "I will give thanks to the Lord." Psalm 7:17

Jesus healed 10 men. How many men are in this picture? _____
How many more men do you need to add to show all the men Jesus healed? _____
Draw that many more men.

These pictures show some times we can say thank you. Find these shapes in the picture: ○ □ △ ▭

When we say thank you we are being kind. We can thank God for the people who help us. The Bible says, "I will give thanks to the Lord." Psalm 7:17

BONUS IDEA! Use red to trace around the biggest ○. Use blue to trace around the smallest △. Use green to trace around the biggest □. Use yellow to trace around the biggest ▭.

Look at the picture to see how much a rich man
in Bible times may have had.

Make one tally mark for each item you count.
Write the number on the line below your tally marks.

Jesus told a rich man to share with poor people. Jesus wants us to share, too. The Bible
says, "Do good and be ready to share." (See 1 Timothy 6:18.)

**BONUS
IDEA!**   Think of something you can share with others.

Draw lines to connect the capital letters with the small letters. You will match each item with a picture of how to share.

A

B

C

D

c

a

d

b

Sharing is a way to obey God and do good. It feels good to share, too!
The Bible says, "Do good and be ready to share." (See 1 Timothy 6:18.)

BONUS IDEA!

Draw a picture of something you can share with someone. Write its name.

Trace the path to the city.
Follow this pattern:

Start

palm branch   coat   Jesus

The people sang praises to Jesus as He rode into Jerusalem.
We can praise Jesus, too. The Bible says, "How good it is to
sing praises to our God." Psalm 147:1

BONUS IDEA!

Draw 3 pictures. Use them in a pattern to make a path.
Give it to a friend to trace.

Trace the path to the city.
Follow this pattern:

Start

palm branch   coat   Jesus

The people sang praises to Jesus as He rode into Jerusalem.
We can praise Jesus, too. The Bible says, "How good it is to
sing praises to our God." Psalm 147:1

BONUS IDEA! Draw 3 pictures. Use them in a pattern to make a path.
Give it to a friend to trace.

Color the picture to find a hidden name.

◯ = red   △ = blue

We can thank God for Jesus by singing songs about Him. The Bible says, "How good it is to sing praises to our God." Psalm 147:1

BONUS IDEA!

Write the name **JESUS** on the spaces.

_____ _____ _____ _____ _____

Color the picture by using the correct colored crayon for each numbered space.

1-GREEN   2-BROWN   3-GRAY   4-YELLOW

The tomb is empty. God made Jesus alive again! The Bible says, "Jesus is risen from the dead." (See Matthew 28:7.) We can thank God that Jesus is alive.

BONUS IDEA! Draw a ◯ around JESUS' name every place you find it in this puzzle.

J	E	S	U	S	R	J
E	J	E	S	U	S	E
S	K	J	E	S	U	S
U	B	V	U	E	P	U
S	U	S	E	J	C	S

Find and circle these things in the picture.

In the spring, we can be thankful for plants and animals. But most of all, we can thank God that Jesus is alive! The Bible says, "Jesus is risen from the dead." (See Matthew 28:7.)

BONUS IDEA!

○ something that is to the ◁LEFT of the 🐕.

☐ something that is to the RIGHT▷ of the 🐦.

Color something that you thank God for.

Draw lines to connect the 3 things that belong in each group.

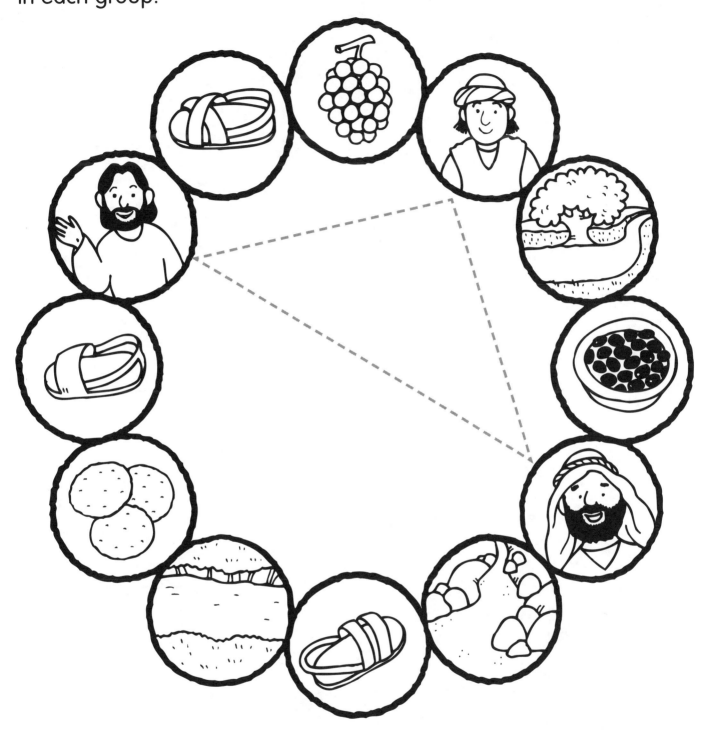

Jesus walked and talked with His friends. They were glad Jesus was with them. Jesus is with us, too. The Bible says, "Thanks be to God for Jesus." (See 2 Corinthians 9:15.)

BONUS IDEA! Use the same color to color each group of 3 pictures. Then draw 1 more picture that belongs with each group.

Fill in the blanks with the missing letters to find out the places these pictures show.

_ake   t_ee

_ark

_oo

ountain

yar_

_chool

We can thank God that Jesus is with us everywhere we go. The Bible says, "Thanks be to God for Jesus." (See 2 Corinthians 9:15.)

BONUS IDEA!

Draw a picture of a place you have been.

139

Draw the missing lines in the picture.

We can thank God for the good news that Jesus is alive! The Bible tells us, "Jesus said, 'I am alive for ever and ever!'" (See Revelation 1:18.)

BONUS IDEA!

How many lines did you draw in? _____
Cut this picture into that many pieces to make a puzzle.

The children in the pictures are happy to tell the good news that Jesus is alive. Connect the pictures to show who each child talks to.

The Bible says, "Jesus said, 'I am alive for ever and ever!'" (See Revelation 1:18.)
We can share the good news that Jesus is alive with others.

BONUS IDEA!

Use the code to finish the message.

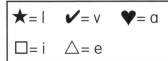

★ = l   ✔ = v   ♥ = a
□ = i   △ = e

Jesus is ___ ___ ___ ___ ___ .
         ♥   ★   □   ✔   △

Draw a line to connect all the boxes with pictures of people.
Don't go through any box that doesn't have a person in it.

Paul told the good news about Jesus' love to many people. We can tell other people about Jesus' love, too. The Bible tells us, "Jesus said, 'Go and tell the good news.'" (See Mark 16:15.)

BONUS IDEA!

How many people are wearing something on their head? _____ Color them RED.
How many people are not? _____ Color them BROWN.

Circle the person in each row who is different.

We can listen to the good news about Jesus' love and then tell it to someone else.
The Bible tells us, "Jesus said, 'Go and tell the good news.'" (See Mark 16:15.)

BONUS IDEA!

Below each letter write the letter that comes after it in the alphabet.

f	n	n	c

m	d	v	r

You wrote good news! Draw a ◯ around those words in the Bible verse.

Look at the pictures of Paul and Silas singing in jail.
Color the 2 pictures that are exactly the same.

Paul and Silas sang songs to God and thanked Him. We can sing songs that tell about God and all He has done, too. The Bible says, "Sing to God; tell of all his wonderful acts." (See Psalm 105:2.)

BONUS IDEA!

Make up a song about God or sing a song you know about God.

We can use music to tell about Jesus and His love.
○ these children in the picture.

We can sing songs about all the wonderful things Jesus has done.
The Bible says, "Sing to God; tell of all his wonderful acts." (See Psalm 105:2.)

BONUS IDEA!

Use two pencils to tap a musical beat while you say the words of the Bible verse.
Teach your beat to a friend.

Color 1 square in the chart for each item of that kind that you see in the picture.

	1	2	3	4	5	6	7

Paul obeyed God's Word and told others about Jesus. We can obey God's Word, too. The Bible says, "I will obey God's word." (See Psalm 119:17.)

Color all stripes that go **up and down** ||||| RED.

Color all the stripes that go **across** ≡ BLUE.

Look at each number. Then find the letter in the secret code that has the same number of dots. Write that letter on the line above the number.

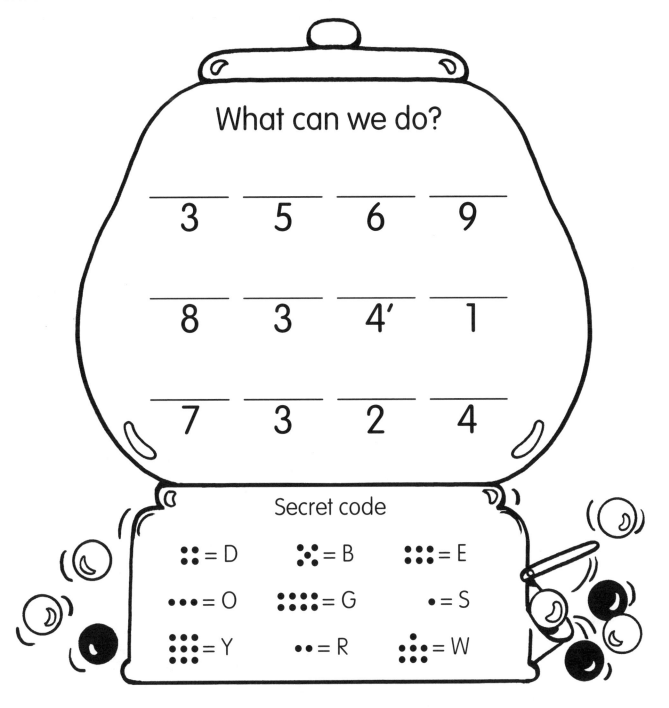

What can we do?

___ ___ ___ ___
3   5   6   9

___ ___ ___ ___
8   3   4' 1

___ ___ ___ ___
7   3   2   4

Secret code

⠿ = D   ⠿ = B   ⠿ = E

••• = O   ⠿ = G   • = S

⠿ = Y   •• • = R   ⠿ = W

The Bible is God's Word. The Bible says, "I will obey God's word." (See Psalm 119:17)
"I will obey God's word." (See Psalm 119:17.)

BONUS IDEA!

Draw a △ around "I" in the verse.   Draw a ☁ around "God's" in the verse.

Draw an ◯ around "will" in the verse.   Draw a ▢ around "word" in the verse.
                                            Read the verse.

Help Paul's nephew find his way to warn the prison guards. Then help the guards take Paul out of the city.

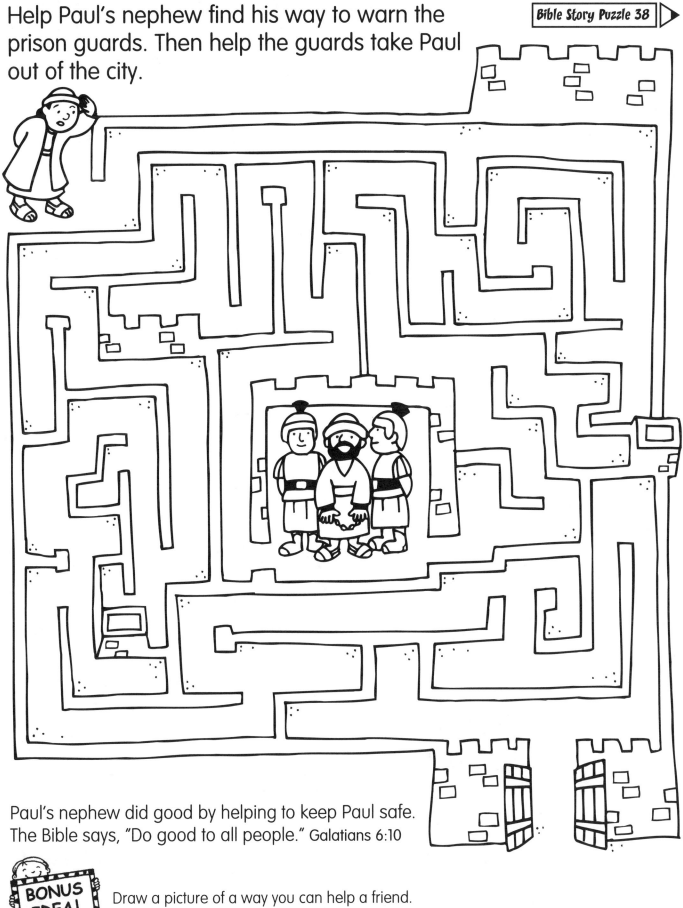

Paul's nephew did good by helping to keep Paul safe. The Bible says, "Do good to all people." Galatians 6:10

BONUS IDEA! Draw a picture of a way you can help a friend.

Circle 5 things that are different. Tell a good thing someone in the picture is doing.

We can do good things to help people. The Bible says, "Do good to all people." Galatians 6:10

Write how many are in the picture.

   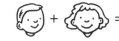

Color in everything in this picture that starts with an **S** or a **B**. There are at least 6 things to color.

Paul showed God's love to his friends in a shipwreck. We can show God's love to our friends, too. The Bible says, "A friend loves at all times." Proverbs 17:17

BONUS IDEA! Draw some things that start with a **T** sound.

Follow the color key to color the picture.

Color Key

Red

Yellow

Green

Blue

Purple

When we are kind to our friends we are showing love.
The Bible says, "A friend loves at all times." Proverbs 17:17

☐ the word that tells what this child is doing.

BONUS IDEA!

laugh   share   sing

Follow the **E**'s to show Joseph's path to Egypt.

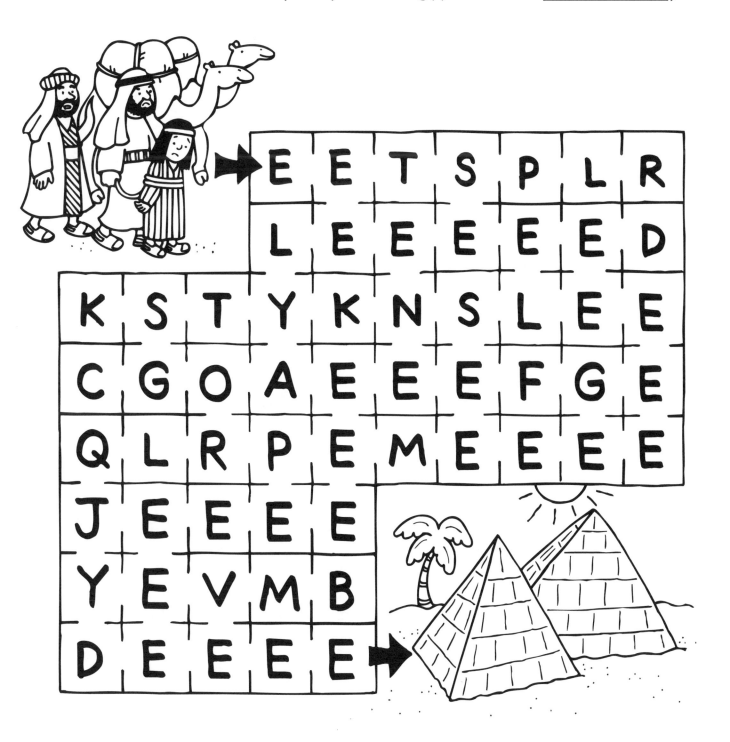

| E | E | T | S | P | L | R |
| L | E | E | E | E | E | D |

K	S	T	Y	K	N	S	L	E	E
C	G	O	A	E	E	E	F	G	E
Q	L	R	P	E	M	E	E	E	E
J	E	E	E	E
Y	E	V	M	B
D	E	E	E	E

God was with Joseph when Joseph was taken to Egypt. God is with us, too. The Bible says, "The Lord your God will be with you wherever you go." Joshua 1:9

BONUS IDEA!

Find the word **GO** in the maze. Copy the word.
Then add a **D** to the end of it. Now you've spelled **GOD**!

Here are things you might take on a trip. Circle the two things in each row that are exactly the same.

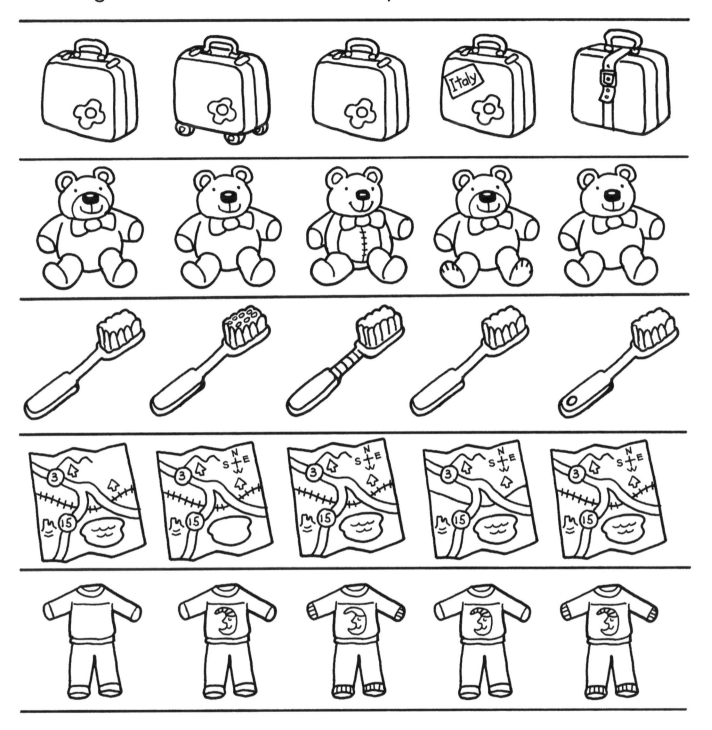

God is with us when we take trips, stay at home—everywhere. The Bible says, "The Lord your God will be with you wherever you go." Joshua 1:9

BONUS IDEA!

Draw something inside the suitcase that you take on a trip.

Use BLUE to color each object in the groups of 8 or **more**. Use ORANGE to color each object in the groups of 7 or **less**.

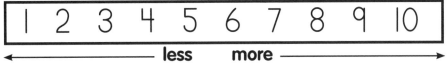

less   more

Joseph did what was right. God will help us do what is right, too. The Bible says, "Don't get tired of doing what is right." (See 2 Thessalonians 3:13.)

BONUS IDEA!

Count how many pictures there are on the page. _____
Write a number by each picture if you need help keeping track.

Trace the line from each child to the picture of the right choice.

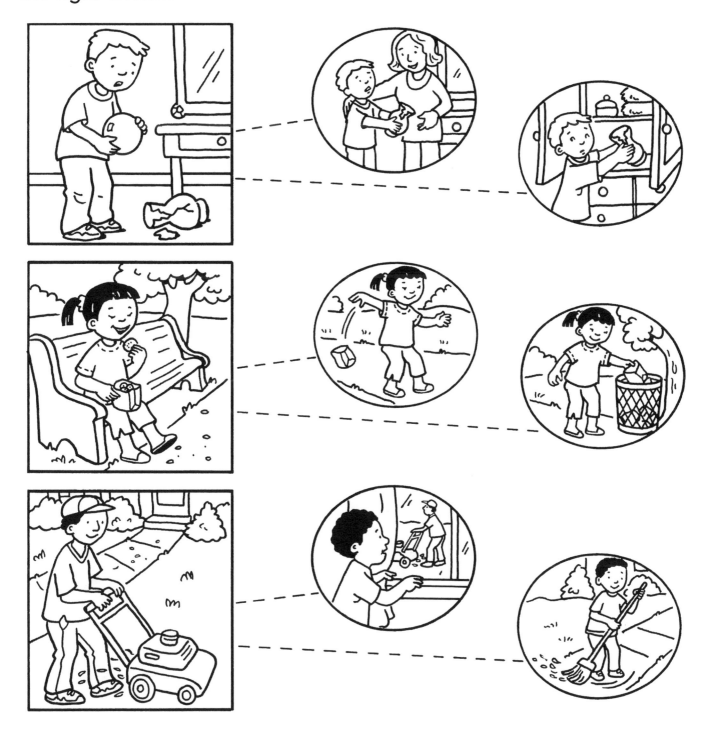

God helps us choose to do right. The Bible says, "Don't get tired of doing what is right."
(See 2 Thessalonians 3:13.)

BONUS IDEA!

Cross out the shapes and pictures. Write the letters that are left in the space to finish the sentence.

△	❀	r	☐	◯	🐘	i	▭	g	🕷	❁	h	🌱	t

Do what is _____ _____ _____ _____ _____ .

Draw a ◯ around the items hidden in the picture.

God helped Joseph save food to share. God can help us share with others, too.
The Bible says, "Share with God's people who are in need." Romans 12:13

Find 5 letters in the picture.
Draw a line to connect the letters to spell the word SHARE.

Find out what each child is sharing. Draw a line to match each piece to where it fits in a picture.

We can help others by sharing. The Bible says, "Share with God's people who are in need." Romans 12:13

BONUS IDEA! Draw a picture of someone you can share with.

Count each set and write the number. Then draw
lines connecting the sets of the same number.

1 2 3 4 5 6 7 8 9 10

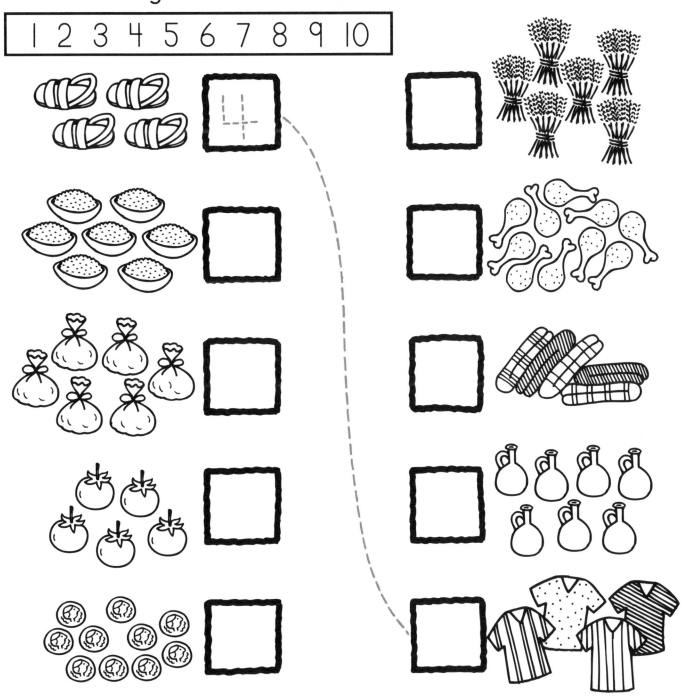

Joseph forgave his family. He showed love for them by giving them what they needed.
God helps us show His love to others. The Bible says, "Love one another." John 13:34

BONUS IDEA!

Count the items in the sets above
to complete these number sentences.

Circle 10 things that don't belong.

These family members are showing love to each other. The Bible says, "Love one another." John 13:34. They are doing what the Bible says.

Finish the sentence telling something you can do to show love to your family.

I can _____ .

In each row, draw the pictures to complete the pattern. | Bible Story Puzzle 44 ▷

God cared for Elijah by giving him food to eat and water to drink. God loves and cares for us, too. The Bible says, "God has been good to me." (See Genesis 33:11.)

BONUS IDEA! Make a sound pattern by clapping your hands and tapping your legs.
Try this pattern: tap/tap/clap, tap/tap/clap.
What other patterns can you make?

Draw lines to match the times of day with things you do at that time.

morning

afternoon

evening

night

God knows what we need all day long. He takes care of us. The Bible says, "God has been good to me." (See Genesis 33:11.)

BONUS IDEA!

◯ something in the pictures that you need.

© 2010 Gospel Light. Permission to photocopy granted to the original purchaser only. *The Big Book of Preschool Puzzles #2.*

183

Draw a ◯ around the flour and oil jugs that match the widow's.

The widow was afraid of having no food. God helped the widow have food. God helps us when we're afraid, too. The Bible tells us, "God said, 'Do not be afraid, for I am with you.'" (See Genesis 26:24.)

BONUS IDEA!

On the blank lines write the beginning sound of each picture to find a great thing to remember:

God is __ __ __ __ __ __ .

Draw a line through the storm maze to help the child get to someone God gave to help him.

God is with us when we are afraid. We can ask Him for help. The Bible says, "God said, 'Do not be afraid, for I am with you.'" (See Genesis 26:24.)

BONUS IDEA!

Trace the letters of the thank-You prayer.

Thank You, God

Color in the spaces with numbers to see 4 things in Elisha's new room.

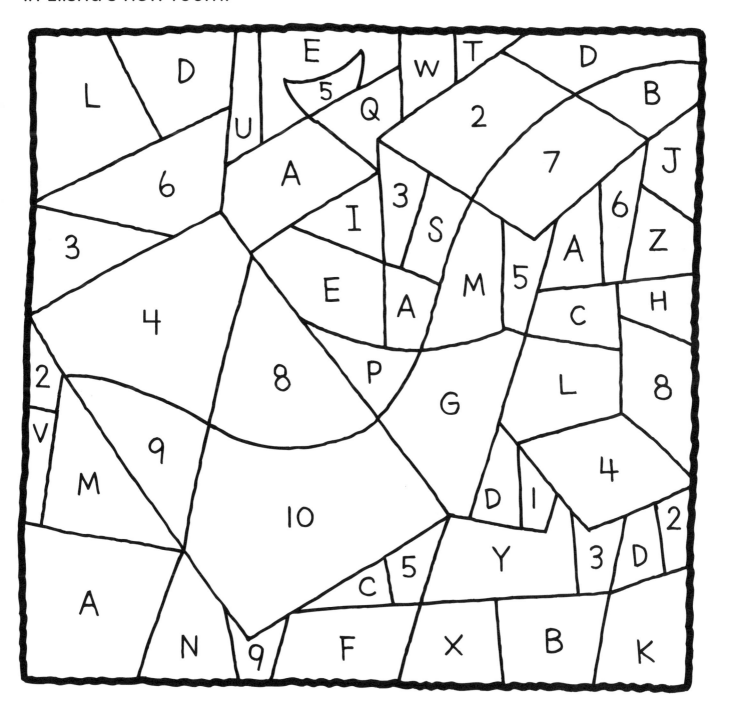

A kind woman and her husband made a room for Elisha. God cared for Elisha. God cares for us and gives us what we need. The Bible says, "God gives us what we need." (See Philippians 4:19.)

BONUS IDEA! Draw a picture of 4 things in your room. Thank God for giving you what you need!

Circle the things in the picture that start with the letter **B**.

Who is helping this family have what they need. God helps us have what we need. The Bible says, "God gives us what we need." (See Philippians 4:19.)

BONUS IDEA! Draw or write something that a baby needs.

Draw lines to match each shadow to its shape in the picture.

God showed His power by making Naaman well. God is powerful and can help us, too! The Bible says, "Lord, you are great and powerful." (See Jeremiah 10:6.)

BONUS IDEA!

God showed His power when Naaman went into the river 7 times. Say the word **powerful** 7 times, as fast as you can.

Count the hidden ◯, ☐ and △. Write the numbers in the spaces.

◯ = _____   ☐ = _____   △ = _____

God made many powerful things. The Bible says, "Lord, you are great and powerful." (See Jeremiah 10:6.)

BONUS IDEA!

☐ the words that start with same letter in each row.

wind	rain	whale	waves
elephant	egg	horse	apple
tree	cow	tulip	tomato

Draw a ○ around each object when you find it in the picture below.

God helped the Israelites when they were crossing a big river. God helps us, too. The Bible says, "The Lord is my helper; I will not be afraid." Hebrews 13:6

BONUS IDEA!

Trace these letters to remind you of what God does for you. Then find these letters hidden in the picture above!

help

Draw lines to match the things that rhyme.
◯ the pictures that might be scary.

When we feel afraid, we ask God to help us. The Bible says, "The Lord is my helper; I will not be afraid." Hebrews 13:6

BONUS IDEA!

What can you do when you are afraid? Use the code to write what you can do in the spaces.

Write the missing numbers in the □s.

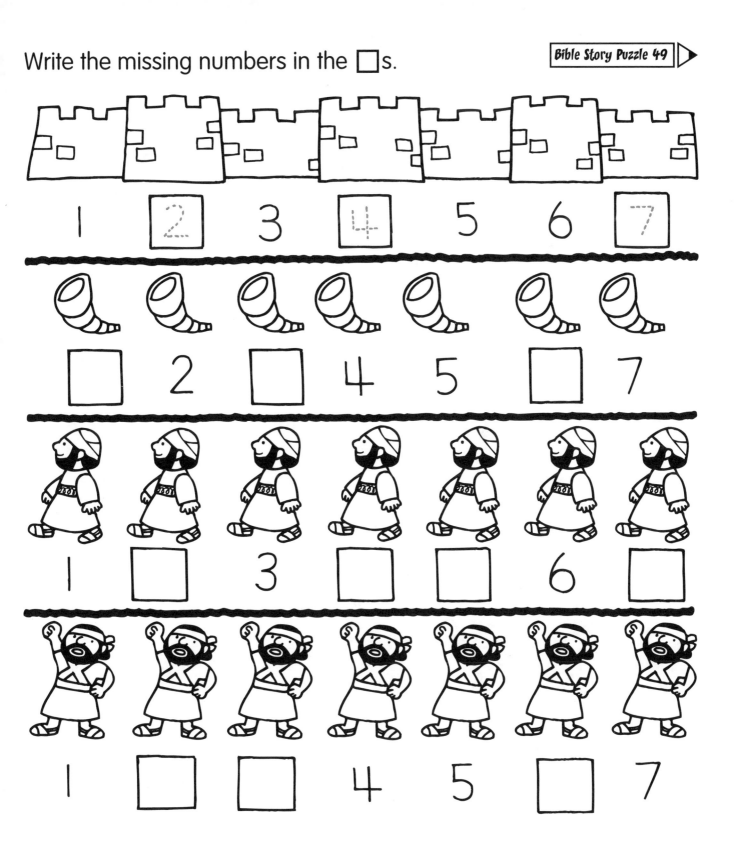

1 2 3 4 5 6 7

□ 2 □ 4 5 □ 7

1 □ 3 □ □ 6 □

1 □ □ 4 5 □ 7

God made the walls of Jericho fall down. Joshua trusted in God. The Bible says, "I trust in the Lord." Psalm 31:6

BONUS IDEA! Color 3 🎺 s YELLOW. Color 4 🚶 s GREEN. Color 5 🙌 s RED.

Go through the maze to connect each child with what he or she wants to play with.

God helps us every day. The Bible says, "I trust in the Lord." Psalm 31:6

BONUS IDEA!

Write a sentence about something you like to do.
Tell God thank-You for helping you each day.

203

Draw a palm tree in the box by following the steps.

1. Draw

2. Add

3. Add

4. Add

Deborah obeyed God's words. She helped other people obey God, too. The Bible says, "Hear the word of God and obey it." Luke 11:28

BONUS IDEA!

Draw 4 lines to make a ☐.
Make your ☐ look like a Bible.
Tell someone 1 thing that God's Word, the Bible, says to do.

Circle the words hidden in the puzzle.
Look across and down.

listen   share   help

be kind   obey   hug

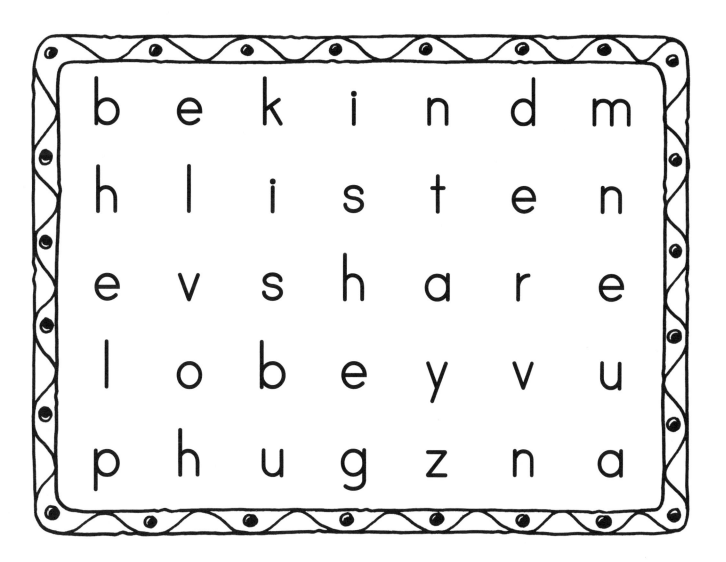

```
b e k i n d m
h l i s t e n
e v s h a r e
l o b e y v u
p h u g z n a
```

We are obeying when we listen to God's Word and do what it says.
The Bible says, "Hear the word of God and obey it." Luke 11:28

BONUS IDEA!

Draw lines to match the body part to the word that tells what it does.

    see

👁   hear

👄   taste

Count each kind of object in the picture.
Write the correct number next to each object.

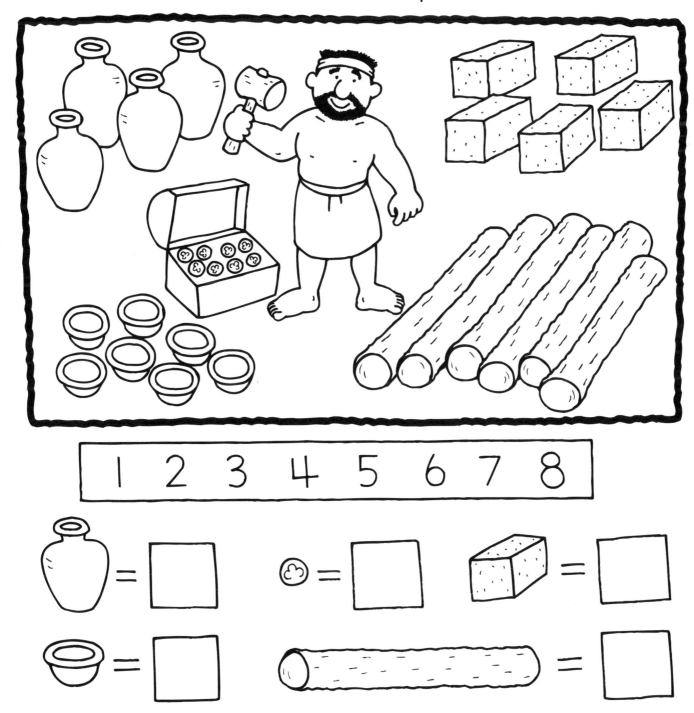

Joash helped God's people obey God by fixing the Temple. We can learn from other people what God wants us to do, too. The Bible says, "Teach me your way, O Lord."
Psalm 27:11

BONUS IDEA!   Write the beginning letter on each object.

Draw a path through the maze. Write the words you pass on the lines.

We can learn from others what God's Word, the Bible, says. The Bible says, "Teach me your way, O Lord." Psalm 27:11

BONUS IDEA! On a separate paper, write a prayer to God. Begin your prayer by writing, "Dear God."

Draw a ⭕ around the little pictures that are part of the big picture. Draw an ✖ on the little pictures that are not part of the big picture.

Queen Esther did good by helping God's people stay safe. God helps us be ready to do good. The Bible says, "Be ready to do whatever is good." Titus 3:1

BONUS IDEA!

Draw a ⭕ around all the objects in the picture that start with a **G**.

Draw lines to match each circled object in the big picture with a small picture. The small pictures show ways to help.

When we help others we are doing good. The Bible says, "Be ready to do whatever is good." Titus 3:1

BONUS IDEA!

Count the pinecones in the picture. Write the number here: _____

Bible Story Index (in Bible order)

Old Testament

New Testament

Bible Verse Index (in Bible order)

Skills Index

Mazes

Numbers (Math Readiness)

Observation Skills

Reading Readiness

Shapes